At the Seaside

in pictures

Pictures
to share

For Rachel.
My supporter
and best friend.

**Pictures
to share**

Published in 2014 by Pictures to Share Community Interest Company,
a UK based social enterprise that publishes illustrated books for older people.

www.picturestoshare.co.uk

ISBN: 978-0-9563818-7-3

Front cover: Silver Morning, Aldeburgh, 1932 Algernon Talmage (1871-1939). Oil on canvas.
               Bridgeman Images

Endpapers: Shells © Universal History Archive/UIG / Science & Society Picture Library
               - All rights reserved.

Title page: Two young girls holding dolls and a bucket and spade lean out of a railway carriage
               window as they depart for their summer holiday from Euston Station, London.
               Fred Morley / Hulton Archive / Getty Images

At the Seaside

in pictures

Edited by Helen J Bate

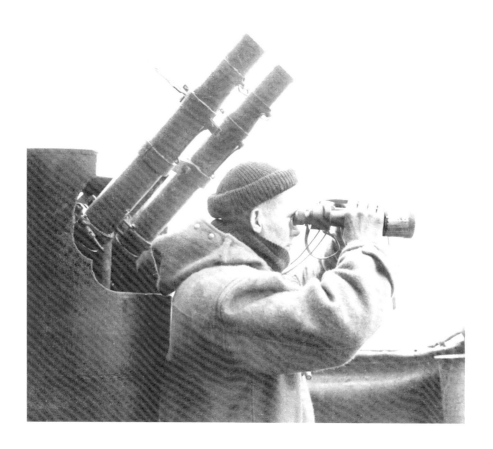

Nowhere in the UK is more than 70 miles from the coast.

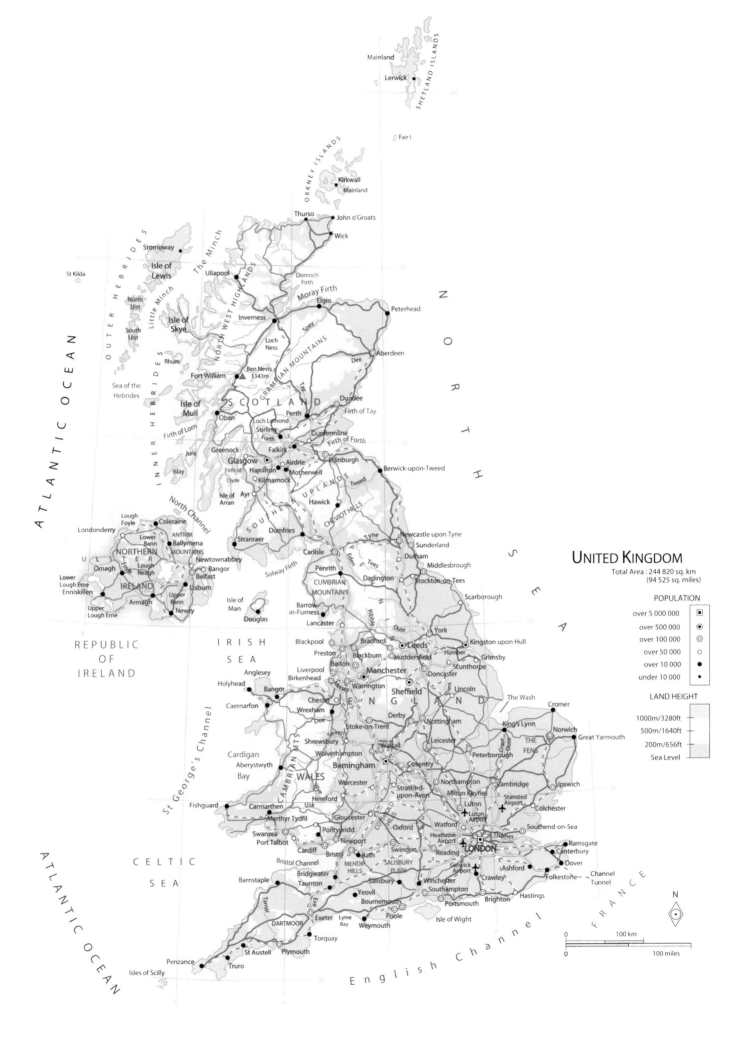

Mainland

SHETLAND ISLANDS

Lerwick

Fair I.

ORKNEY ISLANDS
Kirkwall
Mainland

Thurso   John o'Groats
Wick

Stornoway

OUTER HEBRIDES   The Minch   NORTH
Isle of
Lewis   Ullapool   Dornoch
Firth
St Kilda   Moray Firth
North   NORTH WEST HIGHLANDS   Elgin   Peterhead
Uist   Inverness
Little Minch
Isle of   Loch   Spey
Skye   Ness
South   GRAMPIAN MOUNTAINS   Dee   Aberdeen
Uist
Rhum   Ben Nevis   N
1343m   Tay
Sea of the   Fort William
Hebrides   Dundee   O
INNER HEBRIDES   SCOTLAND   Firth of Tay
Isle of   Perth
Mull   Oban   Loch Lomond   R
Stirling   Dunfermline   T
Forth   Firth of Forth
Firth of Lorn   Greenock   Falkirk   Edinburgh
Jura   Glasgow Airdrie   H
Hamilton Motherwell   Berwick-upon-Tweed
Islay   Firth of   Kilmarnock
Clyde   Tweed   S
Isle of   Ayr
Arran   SOUTHERN UPLANDS   Hawick   E
Lough   Hawick
Foyle   Coleraine   CHEVIOT HILLS   A
Londonderry   ANTRIM   Dumfries
Lower   Ballymena   Tyne   Newcastle upon Tyne
Bann   MOUNTAINS   Stranraer   Sunderland
ULSTER   Newtownabbey   Carlisle   Durham
NORTHERN   Lough   Bangor   Solway Firth   Eden   Tees   Middlesbrough
Omagh   Neagh   Belfast   Penrith   Darlington   Stockton-on-Tees
IRELAND   Lisburn   CUMBRIAN
Lower   MOUNTAINS   Scarborough
Lough Erne   Armagh   Upper   Isle of   Barrow-   N
Enniskillen   Bann   Man   in-Furness
Upper   Newry   Lancaster   York
Lough Erne   Douglas   Ribble   Kingston upon Hull
REPUBLIC   IRISH   Blackpool   Bradford   Leeds
OF   SEA   Preston   Blackburn Huddersfield   Humber   Grimsby
IRELAND   Bolton   Scunthorpe
Liverpool   Manchester   Doncaster   Lincoln
Anglesey   Birkenhead   Warrington   Trent
Holyhead   Sheffield   The Wash   Cromer
Bangor   Chester   ENGLAND
Caernarfon   Wrexham   Derby   Nottingham   King's Lynn   Norwich
Dee   Stoke-on-Trent   Leicester   THE   Great Yarmouth
CAMBRIAN MTS   Severn   FENS
Cardigan   Shrewsbury   Peterborough
Aberystwyth   Wolverhampton   Walsall   Ipswich
Bay   WALES   Birmingham   Coventry   Cambridge
Worcester   Northampton   Stansted   Colchester
Stratford-   Milton Keynes   Airport
Fishguard   upon-Avon
Carmarthen   Hereford   Luton   Southend-on-Sea
Usk   Gloucester   Oxford   Watford   Luton   Thames
Merthyr Tydfil   COTSWOLDS   Airport
Swansea   Pontypridd   Heathrow   LONDON   Ramsgate
Port Talbot   Newport   Swindon   Airport   Canterbury
Cardiff   Bristol   Reading   Gatwick   Dover
Bath   Airport   Ashford   Channel
Bristol Channel   MENDIP   SALISBURY   Crawley   Folkestone   Tunnel
HILLS   PLAIN   Hastings
Barnstaple   Bridgwater   Salisbury   Winchester   Brighton
Taunton   Southampton   Portsmouth
Yeovil   Bournemouth   Poole   Isle of Wight
Exe   Bournemouth   Weymouth
DARTMOOR   Exeter   Lyme
Tamar   Bay
Torquay
St Austell   Plymouth
Penzance   Truro
Isles of Scilly

ATLANTIC OCEAN

REPUBLIC
OF
IRELAND

St George's Channel

CELTIC
SEA

ATLANTIC OCEAN

English Channel

FRANCE

UNITED KINGDOM

Total Area : 244 820 sq. km
(94 525 sq. miles)

POPULATION

over 5 000 000
over 500 000
over 100 000
over 50 000
over 10 000
under 10 000

LAND HEIGHT

1000m/3280ft
500m/1640ft
200m/656ft
Sea Level

N

0   100 km

0   100 miles

We drove down

from the Midlands
to Kent in our old Rover 12
(which didn't do more than 45 mph).

There were no motorways then,
and we drove right through
central London.

It took hours and hours!

But when we caught our
very first glimpse of
the sea in the distance,
we were **so** excited...

...it was magical!

Eastbourne.

An English seaside town in the sunshine.

In August 2003
temperatures of 38.5°Centigrade
(or over 100° Fahrenheit)
were recorded in the
south of England.

Image: Eastbourne, poster advertising British Railways
(colour litho) Bridgeman Images

Sisters.

Whatever you do
they will love you;

even if they
don't love you
they are connected
to you till you die.

You can be boring
and tedious with sisters,
whereas you have
to put on a good face
with friends.

Painting: Detail from Play in the Surf (oil on panel),
Potthast, Edward Henry (1857-1927) / Private Collection /
Photo © Christie's Images / Bridgeman Images

Quotation: Deborah Moggach. Best selling author.

I wish

the whole world
could see what I see.

Sometimes you have
to go up really high
to understand
how small you really are.

What shall we do with the drunken sailor,

What shall we do with the drunken sailor,
What shall we do with the drunken sailor,
Early in the morning.

Hoorah! And up she rises,
Hoorah! And up she rises,
Hoorah! And up she rises,
Early in the morning.

Put him in the guardroom till he gets sober,
Put him in the guardroom till he gets sober,
Put him in the guardroom till he gets sober,
Early in the morning.

Photograph: A group of children trying to refloat the coaster
'Penton' which drifted on to Gorleston beach in Norfolk during gales.
Fred Morley / Hulton Archive / Getty Images

Quotation: Lyrics from popular song. What Shall we do with the Drunken Sailor.

I regard golf

as an expensive way
of playing marbles.

When I was one-and-twenty

I heard a wise man say,

'Give crowns and pounds and guineas
But not your heart away;

Give pearls away and rubies
But keep your fancy free.'

But I was one-and-twenty,
No use to talk to me.

Photograph: Newly weds, honeymooning in Jersey, kiss on the beach.
Haywood Magee/Hulton Archive/Getty Images

Poem: From 'When I was one-and-twenty' by A.E.Houseman (1859 - 1936)

Here in this little Bay,

Full of tumultuous life and great repose,
Where, twice a day,
The purposeless, glad ocean comes and goes,

Under high cliffs,
and far from the huge town,
I sit me down.

For want of me
the world's course will not fail;

When all its work is done, the lie shall rot;
The truth is great, and shall prevail,
When none cares whether it prevail or not.

Painting: Porthmeor Man and Dog (oil on board), Kingsbury,
Alan (Contemporary Artist) / Private Collection / Bridgeman Images

Poem: Magna est Veritas by Coventry Patmore (1823 - 1896)

You Are My Sunshine

My only sunshine.

You make me happy
When skies are grey.

You'll never know, dear,
How much I love you.

Please don't take my sunshine away

Others leave riches
to their children.

I leave
an unsullied reputation.

Happy the man,

and happy he alone,
He who can call today his own:

He who, secure within, can say,
Tomorrow do thy worst,

for I have lived today.

Quotation from Happy the Man by John Dryden 1631 – 1700

The Walrus and
the Carpenter

Were walking close at hand;
They wept like anything to see
Such quantities of sand:

"If this were only cleared away,"
They said, "it would be grand!"

"If seven maids with seven mops
Swept it for half a year.

Do you suppose," the Walrus said,
"That they could get it clear?"

"I doubt it," said the Carpenter,
And shed a bitter tear.

Painting: Magic lantern slide. Alice in Wonderland: Walrus and Carpenter,
1870s. Illustrated by Sir John Tenniel (1820-1914). (Photo by National
Media Museum/SSPL/Getty Images)

Quotation: From The Walrus and the Carpenter by Lewis Carroll, 1832 - 1898

1699
The first
Eddystone
Lighthouse

Designed by
Henry Winstanley
and completed in 1699,
this timber lighthouse was the
first to be built on Eddystone Rocks,
14 miles off the coast of Devon.

A storm one night in 1703
destroyed the lighthouse,
killing the light-keepers,
the workmen and
Winstanley himself. It was
replaced in 1709 by an oak
and iron lighthouse which
survived until 1755 when it
too, was destroyed in a fire.

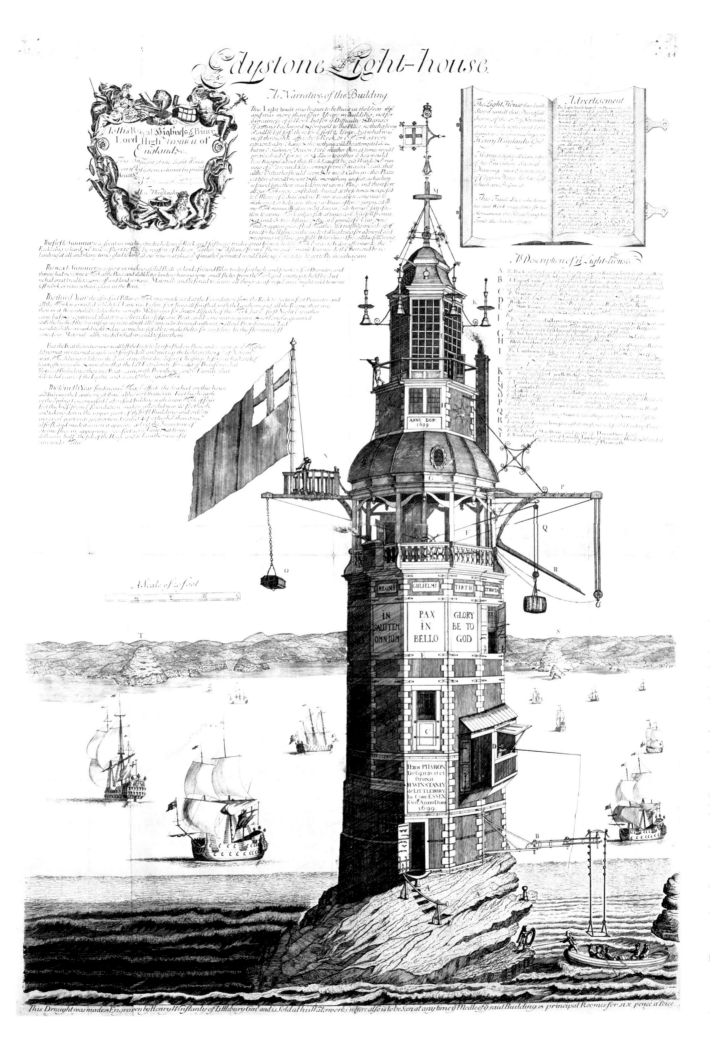

A good friend

is a connection to life;

a tie to the past
and a road to the future.

Photograph: Bathers in 1935 protect their
skins from the sunshine with sun cream.
(William Vanderson/Fox Photos/Getty Images)

Quotation: Lois Wyse 1926 - 2007 American
advertising executive and author.

Bobby Shafto's gone to sea,

Silver buckles at his knee;
He'll come back and marry me,
Bonny Bobby Shafto!

Bobby Shafto's bright and fair,
Panning out his yellow hair;
He's my love for evermore,

Bonny Bobby Shafto!

Punch and Judy shows
first appeared in England
on 9 May 1662

As well as Mr Punch
and his wife Judy,
they usually include a baby,
a crocodile,
a policeman,
a doctor
and a string of sausages.

One, two,
three, four, five,

Once I caught a fish alive.

Six, seven, eight, nine, ten,
Then I let it go again.

Why did you let it go?
Because it bit my finger so.

Which finger did it bite?
This little finger on the right.

They hadna sail'd
a league, a league,
A league but barely three,

When the lift grew dark,
and the wind blew loud,
And gurly grew the sea.

The ankers brak,
and the topmasts lap,
It was sic a deadly storm;

And the waves cam' o'er the broken ship,
Till a' her sides were torn.

Half-owre, half-owre to Aberdour,
'Tis fifty fathoms deep,

And there lies gude Sir Patrick Spens,
Wi' the Scots lords at his feet!

Painting: Rain squall over Covesea Skerries Lighthouse by Jolomo
(John Lowrie Morrison) one of Scotland's best loved contemporart artists.

Poem: From 'Sir Patrick Spens', a popular Scottish traditional 'Child Ballad'

Practice
makes perfect

The Seaside Donkey

Rest is not idleness,
and to lie sometimes
on the grass
under the trees
on a summer's day,
listening to the murmur of water,
or watching the clouds
float across the blue sky,
is by no means
a waste of time.

Painting: Detail from Forty Winks, 1892 (oil on paper), Hall, Fred (1860-1948) / © Penlee House Gallery and Museum, Penzance, Cornwall, UK / Bridgeman Images

Quotation: John Lubbock, "Recreation," The Use of Life, 1894

Wynken, Blynken, and Nod

one night
Sailed off in a wooden shoe,

Sailed on a river of misty light
Into a sea of dew.

'Where are you going,
and what do you wish?'
The old man asked the three.

'We have come to fish
for the herring-fish
That live in this beautiful sea;

Nets of silver and gold have we,

Said Wynken,
Blynken
And Nod.

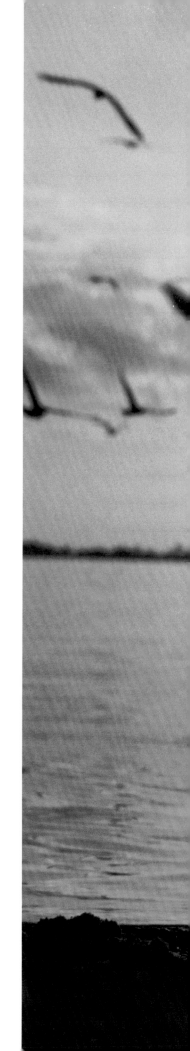

Quotation: From Dutch Lullaby by Eugene Field 1850 - 1895

**Pictures
to share**

Acknowledgements

Our thanks to those contributors who have allowed their text or imagery to be used for a reduced or no fee.

All effort has been made to contact copyright holders. If you own the copyright for work that is represented, but have not been contacted, please get in touch via our website.

Published by

Pictures to Share Community Interest Company.
Tattenhall, Cheshire

www.picturestoshare.co.uk

Printed in England by Langham Press
Foxton, Cambridge CB22 6SA

Graphic design by Duncan Watts

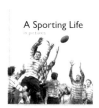

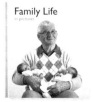

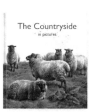

To see our other titles go to
www.picturestoshare.co.uk